F O R :

....

F R O M :

....

Cross*training*

BECOMING YOUR SPIRITUAL BEST

Zondervan*Gifts*

We have a gift for inspiration™

Cross Training: Becoming Your Spiritual Best

Copyright 1999 by ZondervanPublishingHouse

ISBN 0-310-97896-3

Requests for information should be addressed to:
 ZondervanPublishingHouse
Grand Rapids, Michigan 49530
http://www.zondervan.com

Director of Gift Product: Gwen Ellis
Project Editor: Steve Halliday, Crown Media
Design: David Uttley Design
Printed in China

00 01 /HK/ 4 3

Contents

1

Stepping Up to the Line

The LORD is my rock, my fortress and my deliverer;
my God is my rock, in whom I take refuge
He is my shield and the horn of my salvation, my stronghold.

PSALM 18:2

Like every kid who has ever dreamt of being a big leaguer, I wanted to play on a World Series winning team. Naturally, I wanted my final season to end with a bang. However, in my own selfish way, I had forgotten how truly blessed I had been in my career.

Because the Lord had blessed me with good physical health at the beginning of the '94 season, I started dreaming of the World Series ring, the 3000 hits, and the 500 home runs. But God sent me pain in my knee to tell me, "Enough is enough. It's time for you to retire." The Lord had something planned for me beyond the game.

My advice to you is to go when the Lord calls, wherever and whenever he calls. Go whether you understand why he is calling or not. Just go. For each one of us is important to him, and each one of us has a purpose that only he knows.

For all the blessings in my life, I have no one to thank but the Lord.

ANDRE DAWSON, EIGHT-TIME BASEBALL ALL STAR

The problem with most leaders today is they don't stand for anything. Leadership implies movement toward something, and convictions provide that direction. If you don't stand for something, you'll fall for anything.

DON SHULA, FORMER MIAMI DOLPHINS HEAD COACH

The two senior captains for the baseball team invited me to attend a meeting. I didn't know that it was a Fellowship of Christian Athlete's meeting. At that meeting I was presented with a question. What was I going to do with this Man, Jesus Christ? At that point I did decide to accept Jesus Christ as my Savior, and so from that point on it's been a gradual growing process.

SCOTT SANDERSON, FORMER CALIFORNIA ANGELS PITCHER

The LORD is my strength and my song;
he has become my salvation.

EXODUS 15:2

I am not ashamed of the gospel,
because it is the power of God for the salvation of everyone who
believes: first for the Jew, then for the Gentile.

ROMANS 1:16

During his freshman year at college Tim Salmon made friends with a senior catcher named A. C. Martin. "He was a great Christian man," Tim says. "He took me under his wing. He answered most of my questions and helped me understand what it all meant. I came to the point where I realized there was something more than just believing there's a God. It's really wanting to change your life and live for him."

MARK LITTLETON, AUTHOR OF THE *SPORTS HEROES* BOOK SERIES

I wasn't happy going to the gym to practice. The only way to get myself on track . . . to get the bad feelings out of me was to give myself to the Lord. I didn't want to come home and argue with my wife about basketball anymore. It was the best decision in my life.

HERSEY HAWKINS, SEATTLE SUPERSONICS GUARD

Praise be to the God and Father of our Lord Jesus Christ! In his great mercy he has given us new birth into a living hope through the resurrection of Jesus Christ from the dead, and into an inheritance that can never perish, spoil or fade—kept in heaven for you, who through faith are shielded by God's power until the coming of the salvation that is ready to be revealed in the last time. In this you greatly rejoice, though now for a little while you may have had to suffer grief in all kinds of trials. These have come so that your faith—of greater worth than gold, which perishes even though refined by fire—may be proved genuine and may result in praise, glory and honor when Jesus Christ is revealed.

1 PETER 1:3—7

In the spiritual life, we can't save ourselves because we're dead in sin. God can, because he is life. He gives us new life through his death on the cross. He delivers what we can't. He is loyal."

DOUG BOCHTLER, SAN DIEGO PADRES PITCHER

Do good to your servant
according to your word, O LORD.
Teach me knowledge and good judgment,
for I believe in your commands.

PSALM 119:65, 66

For God so loved the world that he gave his one and only Son,
that whoever believes in him shall not perish but have eternal
life. For God did not send his Son into the world to condemn
the world, but to save the world through him.

JOHN 3:16, 17

2

Playing by the Rules

*If anyone competes as an athlete,
he does not receive the victor's crown unless
he competes according to the rules.*

2 TIMOTHY 2:5

There's no place in football for "unnecessary violence," as when a player deliberately hits an opponent in the head or clips him from behind. As a long-standing member of the NFL's Competition Committee, I have championed rules that decrease unnecessary rough play. If I'm remembered for anything as a coach, I hope it's for playing within the rules. I also hope it will be said that my teams showed class and dignity in victory and defeat. It is a source of pride that during my seasons with Miami, the Dolphins were the least-penalized team in the NFL. When my team beats your team, I want it to be fair and square.

DON SHULA, FORMER MIAMI DOLPHINS HEAD COACH

The man of integrity walks securely,
but he who takes crooked paths will be found out.

PROVERBS 10:9

I'm sort of an up-front guy. I think what really defines a man is somebody with strong character. What defines him is not necessarily what the world sees—somebody who can throw a baseball 95 miles per hour or slam-dunk a basketball. What makes a man is how he influences other people.

R.A. DICKEY, TEXAS RANGERS PITCHER

My parents always taught me the right way to handle my anger and pride. Now it comes very naturally. Reading the Bible helps a great deal. I think the Bible outlines clearly how to live your life. I try to live according to Bible standards.

BUCK WILLIAMS, FORMER NBA POWER FORWARD

May integrity and uprightness protect me,
because my hope is in you.

PSALM 25:21

Unfortunately, there are guys in the NFL who take cheap shots and actually try to inflict physical damage on their opponents by taking out their knees or by hitting late. I've had people take cheap shots at me, and it angered me. I don't remember exactly what I've said to people in these circumstances, but suffice it to say that they knew where I stood on the issue. Fortunately, they don't usually do it a second time. I don't do those things. I play hard and hit hard, but I can assure my opponents and fans that I would never do anything to injure anybody intentionally. When I have a chance to make a play, I'll always do it within the rules, and I'll never try to hurt someone with a hit that is technically legal.

It's important to me that I play within the rules, and it's equally important to me that I maintain a reputation as someone who plays clean. I'm very protective of that reputation.

BRYCE PAUP, BUFFALO BILLS OUTSIDE LINEBACKER

Discretion will protect you,
and understanding will guard you.

PROVERBS 2:11

I know, my God,
that you test the heart and are
pleased with integrity.

1 CHRONICLES 29:17

When I was a child, I was always bigger than the other kids. Kids used to call me "Bigfoot" or "Land of the Giant". They'd tease me and run away. Around seventh grade I found something I was good at. I could play football, and I could use my size and achieve success by playing within the rules. I remember telling my mother that someday I would be a professional football player.

REGGIE WHITE, FORMER ALL-PRO DEFENSIVE LINEMAN
FOR THE GREEN BAY PACKERS

In this business, you can quickly go from World Champion to loser, from having a big contract to being released. That's so opposite of God. With him, there was one payment—the death of Jesus Christ. Because of that, there is no need to perform for acceptance. God has already performed. Now we perform out of obedience and thankfulness.

GREG MCMICHAEL, NEW YORK METS PITCHER

I was 22, confused, completely on my own, but when I asked Jesus to take over my life, I had a peace I'd never had before.

The fans in New York have a real passion for baseball, and I think it's okay, even important, for people to have outlets. Playing there is a platform to show them that Christ is my outlet, my provider. The Bronx is a tough place. People are looking for hope. I want to show them that my hope is in God, and theirs can be, too.

JOE GIRARDI, NEW YORK YANKEES CATCHER

*In everything set them an example
by doing what is good.
In your teaching show integrity,
seriousness and soundness of speech that
cannot be condemned,
so that those who oppose you may be
ashamed because they have nothing
bad to say about us.*

TITUS 2:7-8

3

Go for It

Whatever you do,
work at it with all your heart,
as working for the Lord, not for men.

To be a good basketball player, you have to be committed to doing the best you can. You must start with the fundamentals— dribbling, shooting, passing, and defense—and practice more than you want to. I remember that on Friday nights as a young person, when all my friends were getting ready to go out and have fun, I was getting ready to have my fun down at the gym. I wasn't forcing myself to play, but I just loved basketball and couldn't get enough of it. I think that's the key. If you love basketball and really enjoy playing it and if you keep it in the right place behind your relationship with God, your family, and your studies, you'll become the best basketball player you can possibly be.

MARK PRICE, FORMER NBA POINT GUARD

When I play ball, I play aggressively. But that's part of the game. Even trash talk has a place in basketball. But I have my rules for trash talk: no swearing, nothing derogatory about an opponent, and nothing about mothers or sisters. And my best trash talk consists of my "secret" lethal weapon—prayer.

A.C. GREEN, NBA ALL STAR

I think whatever you do in life, if you're consistent at it, you're going to be pretty good, whether it is rebounding, passing, or shooting. And, of course, it takes a lot of hard work and practice.

BUCK WILLIAMS, FORMER NBA POWER FORWARD

The marks of a good player are dedication and a love for the game. A love for what we do. But it's dedication from the perspective that even when it's not fun, you're out there to improve yourself. Love for the game revolves around a desire and a will to play all hours of the day. You have to be dragged off the field. Mom has to call you home. That's what I'd call a real love for the game.

DESMOND ARMSTRONG, SOCCER DEFENDER AND SWEEPER

Football totally consumed my life. I ate, drank, and slept the game. The essence was that it was combat, that one-on-one, man-to-man competition, clean and direct. I was responsible for beating the guy facing me. Pure and simple. It was me against him. No maybes, no gray areas. Either he whups me or I whup him.

There's no question where that taste for combat came from. All those years I followed behind my brothers, they never did *anything* half-speed. When we played football, it was always tackle. Not once did we play touch. When we played baseball, it was never slow-pitch. I remember asking Doug one time to toss me a pitch underhand. I was six years old. He looked at me like I had to be kidding and threw it all the harder for asking.

DENNIS BYRD, FORMER NEW YORK JETS DEFENSIVE LINEMAN

Buy the truth and do not sell it;
get wisdom,
discipline and understanding.

PROVERBS 23:23

The eyes of the LORD
range throughout the earth
to strengthen those whose hearts are
fully committed to him.

2 CHRONICLES 16:9

I was at a church service in my hometown of New Orleans where the pastor preached about being fully committed. He talked about people who are just church-goers, people who aren't fully committed, that they're not reaching their fullest potential as Christians. It really just hit me in my heart. I just got up and said, "I want to change. I want to be a full-time Christian."

AVERY JOHNSON, SAN ANTONIO SPURS POINT GUARD

My commitment to Christ didn't start until my senior year in high school. I was at a youth revival at my church when I knew it was my time to give my whole life to Christ. Since that time, my life hasn't been easy, but he's always there to bring me through when it's tough. Even when things are going great, I have to give him the credit.

MARK PRICE, FORMER NBA POINT GUARD

What most characterizes a true champion is his heart. His will to win. His resolve to train. His determination to pay the price. The difference lies in the heart.

A man once went to his high school reunion, accompanied by his twenty-year-old son. He could hardly wait to find his old football coach and show off his muscular son, who was now playing college ball.

After introducing his son, the beaming father asked the coach, "Who is the bigger man?"

The coach looked at the aging man, now bald and bulging. Then at his growing, bulky son. Clearly the son was now bigger, taller, and stronger.

But the coach suddenly grabbed the father's chest, clutching his shirt right over his heart. He said, "This is how I still measure a man. By his heart."

STEVEN J. LAWSON, PASTOR AND AUTHOR OF *MEN WHO WIN*

Let us draw near
to God with a sincere heart
in full assurance of faith.

HEBREWS 10:22

4

Going the Extra Mile

All hard work brings a profit.

PROVERBS 14:23

They say I came out of nowhere my senior season at Mustang, and in a way it was true. I had played hardly any varsity football at all. I had never started a game. There had been no newspaper stories written about me, no headlines, no films or scouting reports filed in coaches' offices at other schools. Other schools didn't even know I existed. So when I started making waves that fall of 1983, people were stunned, even people in Mustang. They were asking themselves, "Is this the same kid?"

But I wasn't surprised. I knew I had put in more time than anybody else. If somebody was going to beat me, he was going to have to have worked harder than I had, and I didn't think that was possible. I knew how much I could give, how deep I could reach. I'd answered all those questions myself.

DENNIS BYRD, FORMER NEW YORK JETS DEFENSIVE LINEMAN

You have to get up each morning with a clear goal in mind saying to yourself, "Today I'm going to do my best in every area. I'm not going to take the easy way; I'm going to give 100 percent."

TOM LANDRY, FORMER DALLAS COWBOYS COACH

But by the grace of God I am what I am, and his grace to me was not without effect. No, I worked harder than all of them—yet not I, but the grace of God that was with me.

1 CORINTHIANS 15:10

We also rejoice in our sufferings,
because we know that suffering
produces perseverance;
perseverance, character;
and character, hope.

ROMANS 5:3-4

I have worked much harder, been in prison more frequently, been flogged more severely, and been exposed to death again and again. Five times I received from the Jews the forty lashes minus one. Three times I was beaten with rods, once I was stoned, three times I was shipwrecked, I spent a night and a day in the open sea, I have been constantly on the move. I have been in danger from rivers, in danger from bandits, in danger from my own countrymen, in danger from Gentiles; in danger in the city, in danger in the country, in danger at sea; and in danger from false brothers. I have labored and toiled and have often gone without sleep; I have known hunger and thirst and have often gone without food; I have been cold and naked. Besides everything else, I face daily the pressure of my concern for all the churches.

2 CORINTHIANS 11:23-28

Sometimes I was the hero. Sometimes I wasn't. I found out that trying to please everybody—my parents, friends, coach, and the media—was impossible.

I had a Christian roommate who played football and he helped me, reminded me of Colossians 3:23 ("Whatever you do, work at it with all your heart, as working for the Lord."). It helped me take my eyes off what I was doing and put them on the Lord. I realized it doesn't matter what others think, it matters what God thinks. So that's what I try to do with everything in life—please the Lord. Everything else doesn't matter.

BRENT PRICE, NBA POINT GUARD

You have to set your mind to the hard work. Above all, you must get really familiar with the soccer ball. You have to learn to control it. Learn to juggle—keep the ball in the air with your feet, your thighs, your head. I always heard from soccer players and coaches that the "soccer ball is your best coach." Get to know the soccer ball, how you control it with your chest and thighs. Touch it as many ways and times as you can.

PHILIP WOLF, SOCCER MIDFIELDER

*May the Lord direct your hearts into God's love
and Christ's perseverance.*

2 THESSALONIANS 3:5

My first season in the NFL taught me a lot about preparation, about being ready when you're called on to perform. While I was on the injured list, it would have been easy to just kick back and wait until I was activated to get ready to play. The encouragement from my coaches and teammates led me to stay involved in what the team was doing and to make that a priority. I worked out, I practiced, and I studied. When my opportunity came to play, I was ready.

God also taught me a lot about resting in him when things don't go my way.

BRYCE PAUP, BUFFALO BILLS OUTSIDE LINEBACKER

We work hard with our own hands.
When we are cursed, we bless; when we are persecuted,
we endure it; when we are slandered,
we answer kindly.

1 CORINTHIANS 4:12–13

5

Winners Do It

*Therefore I do not run like a man running aimlessly;
I do not fight like a man beating the air. No, I beat my body and
make it my slave so that after I have preached to others,
I myself will not be disqualified for the prize.*

In the ancient Olympic and Isthmian games, an athlete would begin training ten months before the race. A long-distance runner would submit to rigorous discipline. He would undergo disciplined eating and sleeping habits, an exercise program, and his daily running routine. His goal was clear, his purpose sure: to hone his body into the best possible shape to run. To win.

Then, one month before the games, this athlete would move to Corinth, ten miles from where the Isthmian games were held. There he would submit to training under the watchful eye of a personal coach. This training meant early rising and long days spent in lifting weights, rigorous exercise, and pushing himself to the limit. All this to prepare for the games and to run the famous marathon.

Any success experienced was due, in largest measure, to the intensity of his preparation.

STEVEN J. LAWSON, PASTOR AND AUTHOR OF *MEN WHO WIN*

I knew I was going to have to get bigger and stronger if I was going to excel. So that spring, I devoted myself to weight lifting.

Dad helped me out by allowing me to use one of our old chicken coops—minus the chickens—as a weight room. Brad and I went through the unpleasant task of cleaning it out before we could move in the weights and bench. Talk about a horrible smell! I had built the bench in shop class, and I bought the weights from the high school because no one was using them. Then Brad and I, along with Troy Mount, a friend from Churdan, started working out.

Throughout my high school years, I'd never gotten all that serious about lifting weights. Mostly, I just tinkered around in the high school weight room on its universal machines. I'd go with my buddies and lift two or three days in a row, then I wouldn't lift for a month. Then I'd go lift two or three days in a row again, thinking I was doing myself some good.

In high school, lifting weights was more of an ego thing to me than a way to improve in football. I wanted to be bigger and stronger than other people, and I wanted to look good. I wanted to drive around in my Camaro and be able to hang my big, muscular arm out the window to impress the ladies. Up to that point, I had to smash my arm down on the edge of the car to make it look big. I was heading off to college to play football, and I knew that I'd have to work harder to succeed in college football. It was time for some serious priority setting. I would have to get serious about lifting.

BRYCE PAUP, BUFFALO BILLS OUTSIDE LINEBACKER

For attaining wisdom and discipline;
for understanding words of insight;
for acquiring a disciplined and prudent life,
doing what is right and just and fair;
for giving prudence to the simple,
knowledge and discretion to the young—
let the wise listen and add to their learning,
and let the discerning get guidance—
for understanding proverbs and parables,
the sayings and riddles of the wise.
The fear of the LORD
is the beginning of knowledge,
but fools despise wisdom and discipline.

PROVERBS 1:2-7

My father taught me everything. He taught me how to be a husband, how to be a father, how to work. He worked sixty years without a vacation. He just taught me about working hard and being the best you can be and putting that extra effort into things. A lot of self-discipline stuff. My dad was not an athlete. He only had a sixth grade education. But he knew stuff about the Lord and just life in general.

AVERY JOHNSON, SAN ANTONIO SPURS POINT GUARD

If God is for us, who can be against us? He who did
not spare his own Son, but gave him up for us all—how
will he not also, along with him, graciously give us all things?
Who will bring any charge against those whom God has chosen? It is
God who justifies. Who is he that condemns? Christ Jesus, who
died—more than that, who was raised to life—is at the right hand
of God and is also interceding for us. Who shall separate us from
the love of Christ? Shall trouble or hardship or persecution or
famine or nakedness or danger or sword? As it is written:
"For your sake we face death all day long;
we are considered as sheep to be slaughtered."
No, in all these things we are more than conquerors
through him who loved us.

ROMANS 8:31-37

I think the one benefit that a Christian has over a non-Christian is you can have self-discipline. You are not a slave to the flesh but you can be a slave to righteousness and have control. You can say no to drugs. You can say no to premarital sex. You can say no to dating so you can go to the gym and work on your game. You don't have anything that latches hold to you and controls you that a non-believer would. It is so much easier to be disciplined and work. Put God first and work on your athletic goal. I think the difference between a lot of people and myself is that I worked like it depended on me, and prayed like it depended on God.

DAVID WOOD, FORMER NBA PLAYER

God did not give us a spirit of timidity,
but a spirit of power, of love
and of self-discipline.

2 TIMOTHY 1:7

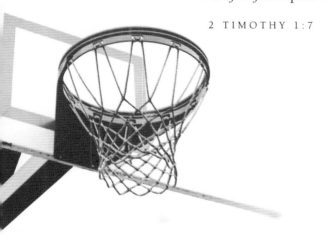

6

Practice Makes Perfect

Everyone who competes in the games
goes into strict training.
1 CORINTHIANS 9:25

Our staff works hard with our players to instill pride in practice performance, giving everything they can in daily practice—the part the crowd and the reporters never see. The concept of practice perfection is difficult for some players to understand. Many times when they go out on the practice field, they're tired or they're beaten up from the previous week's game. There I am, asking them to pick up the tempo, be on top of their play mentally and physically, be sharp in their practice execution. Sometimes these players would rather take the easy way. Like kids, they complain that "none of the other teams practice this hard" or "other teams don't wear pads this often in their practices." Right! Those are usually the teams who have disappointing seasons.

DON SHULA, FORMER MIAMI DOLPHINS HEAD COACH

37

*No discipline seems pleasant
at the time, but painful.
Later on, however,
it produces a harvest of
righteousness and peace for those
who have been trained by it.*

HEBREWS 12:11

The word *discipline* means exercise, training, working out. It actually means to work out in a gym. It comes from the same word from which we have derived the English word *gymnasium*, which literally means to be naked. Discipline originally meant stripping down for the purpose of working out. Young athletes worked out in the nude for freedom of movement, and the gymnasium was the place where they trained. So, discipline came to mean the strenuous training in a gymnasium, which helped the athlete get in shape.

Every successful athlete must train and work out. No exceptions. He must exercise, lift weights, do stretching exercises, sit-ups, pushups, and pull-ups. All to get into shape and keep his muscles toned.

STEVEN J. LAWSON, PASTOR AND AUTHOR OF *MEN WHO WIN*

I had heard a story somewhere about a football player who built up his body by going one-on-one against a billy goat. Day after day he bashed and butted this goat, literally locking horns with this animal to toughen himself up. We didn't have any goats, but the dirt yard outside our family's trailer was nice and flat, a perfect place to put a pole in the ground.

I found a four-by-four green oak post, about six feet long, sunk it about three feet deep and began a routine that became my evening ritual that entire summer. By day I lived in the school's weight room, where Coach Carpenter had just put in a new set of free weights. Then, each night, as the sun was setting and the air was cooling off, I'd go out to that post and settle into a good, solid three-point stance, digging my cleats into the bare earth beneath my feet. Then I'd fire out and slam that wood with my hands or my forearms, using the form and techniques my coaches had taught me. Over and over I hit that post, until the sweat was pouring off me. I'd hit it until my hands actually bled through the calluses that had already formed. Then I'd hit some more. I'd keep going until tears were streaming out of my eyes. That's when I knew it was time to stop, when the pain and exhaustion turned into tears. Only then would I finally drop to the dirt and call it a day. The next night, I'd be back to do it all over again.

DENNIS BYRD, FORMER NEW YORK JETS DEFENSIVE LINEMAN

7

The Cost of Victory

Endure hardship with us like
a good soldier of Christ.
2 TIMOTHY 2:3

The year was 1957. Arkansas and Texas A&M were clashing in the biggest game of the year. The Aggies came to Arkansas undefeated and on a fast track to a coveted national championship. Coached by the legendary Paul "Bear" Bryant, the Aggies boasted the 1957 Heisman Trophy winner and future NFL great John David Crow, as well as other noted players like Gene Stallings and Jack Pardee.

Late in the game, Texas A&M was clinging to a 7-6 lead. The Aggies were driving the length of the field for a second touchdown, which would have sealed the victory and paved the way to the national title. And they were keeping the ball on the ground, thus eating up precious time on the clock. Arkansas was out of time-outs, and time was running out. On all counts, the Razorback cause seemed hopeless.

As A&M was but just a few yards away from the game-clinching touchdown, they lined up with a receiver split wide to the left hash mark. He was covered by a lonely Razorback defender, Don Horton.

Then the unthinkable occurred.

Roddy Osborne, the Aggie quarterback, threw a pass into the left flat. Don Horton, the Arkansas defensive back, gambled all the way and stepped in front of the Aggie receiver. Guessing right, Horton intercepted the pass on the dead run. He was now running full speed with the ball heading for the Razorback end zone!

Before him lay ninety yards of green grass, fame, and glory. A national upset. His name surely would be recorded in Arkansas history for as long as football is played in the Ozarks.

Horton, a high school track star with big-time, blazing speed, set off on the run of his life.

As Horton sprinted down the east sideline, the Arkansas student body was on their feet. Cheering. Hollering. Delirious. The Aggies' national championship crown was about to be denied them.

Suddenly—out of nowhere—came a streaking blur. It was Roddy Osborne, the Aggie quarterback who had thrown the interception. Pursuing all the way across the field, he came running like a madman.

Incredibly, Osborne was narrowing the gap. Osborne, blessed with only average speed (he'd probably consider that a compliment), somehow overtook the lightning-fast Horton at the Aggie eighteen yard line, making the game-saving tackle. Even though Osborne had to run farther, he overtook the faster Horton. No one on the field had possessed the speed to catch Don Horton that day. Yet the slow-footed Osborne ran him down.

Arkansas could not score from the eighteen and Texas A&M hung on to preserve the victory, 7-6, and finish the season number one.

After the game, the reporters huddled around Bear Bryant in the Aggie locker room and asked, "How could Roddy Osborne possibly catch Don Horton?"

As only the Bear could answer, he growled, "Horton was only running for the game-winning touchdown. Osborne was running for his life."

STEVEN J. LAWSON, PASTOR AND AUTHOR OF *MEN WHO WIN*

T he powerful bond between coach and teammates has led not only to commitment, but also to an uncommon self-sacrificing devotion. Each year the team is required to give up something they love. Red meat, candy, fast foods, and movies are a few things players have offered up as a symbol of their sacrificial attitude toward one another.

"It's symbolic of an individual giving up something for the team," says Smith. "It draws the team closer together and is a constant reminder how sacrifice makes a better team."

BOBBIE BRAKER, ON FORMER COACH BRAD SMITH OF THE OREGON CITY PIONEERS HIGH SCHOOL BASKETBALL PROGRAM

Jesus said,
"Suppose one of you wants to build a tower.
Will he not first sit down and estimate the cost
to see if he has enough money to complete it?
For if he lays the foundation and is not able to finish it,
everyone who sees it will ridicule him, saying,
'This fellow began to build and was not able to finish.'
Or suppose a king is about to go to war
against another king. Will he not first sit down
and consider whether he is able with ten
thousand men to oppose the one coming against
him with twenty thousand?
If he is not able, he will send a delegation
while the other is still a long way off and will ask
for terms of peace. In the same way, any of you who does not
give up everything he has cannot be my disciple."

LUKE 14:28-33

Wrestling is an awesome sport to watch. It features strength, surprising speed (at every weight), and no equipment except the wrestlers' physical and mental gifts. College wrestlers work out, they perform, and they sacrifice out of love for the sport.

JOHN CARVALHO, WRITER FOR *SPORTS SPECTRUM* MAGAZINE

I want to know Christ
and the power of his resurrection and the
fellowship of sharing in his sufferings,
becoming like him in his death, and so, somehow,
to attain to the resurrection from the dead.
Not that I have already obtained all this,
or have already been made perfect,
but I press on to take hold of that for which
Christ Jesus took hold of me. Brothers,
I do not consider myself yet to have taken hold of it.
But one thing I do: Forgetting what is behind
and straining toward
what is ahead, I press on toward the goal
to win the prize for which God has called me
heavenward in Christ Jesus.
All of us who are mature
should take such a view of things.
And if on some point you think differently,
that too God will make clear to you.Only let us live
up to what we have already attained.

PHILIPPIANS 3:10-16

8

Putting First Things First

So we make it our goal to please the Lord.
2 CORINTHIANS 5:9

I thank God every time I look back on the 1992 season, for it was then that he taught me that I had to make a priority of giving everything I had thought of as my own—especially my football career—to him. I still had to learn to let God have control in other areas of my life, but after giving my career to him, he blessed me beyond anything I thought was possible.

Before I decided to give God control of my career, I had been struggling along, worrying over where it was going to lead me. I made a mess of it. I nearly ruined it. I was miserable. I wasn't enjoying my lifelong dream of playing professional football.

Since I hadn't given football to God, it became an idol to me. In a way that I hadn't fully realized, I had put football before my Lord. Well, God wasn't about to let that happen, so he let me go on my own. It was like he was saying, "Here, I'll show you what you can do by yourself."

God has been gracious to me at the same time. He not only took the mess I had made of my career and taught me how to quit worrying over it, but he cleaned up that mess and blessed me with success in the career he had chosen for me.

BRYCE PAUP, BUFFALO BILLS OUTSIDE LINEBACKER

It was tempting to forget about living one day at a time. I could easily have zeroed in on my goal, forgetting about everything else.

That is why, before the Friday game, I took time to pray. I asked the Lord, not for success, but for clarity. I asked that he would either swing the door to the major leagues wide open, or slam it shut. I didn't want the ambiguous. My desire to succeed was so strong I thought I might push myself into a situation I wasn't really ready for, either physically or spiritually. I prayed that God would keep directing my path.

DAVE DRAVECKY, FORMER SAN FRANCISCO GIANTS PITCHER

The only thing that counts is faith
expressing itself through love.

GALATIANS 5:6

To have a personal relationship with Jesus Christ has been phenomenal in my life. I often wonder why I make some decisions. Well, it's not me making them, but God is really taking control in my life and sort of steering me in the right direction when it comes time to make decisions. I always tell people who are asking, "Buck, how can you stay injury-free, and how do you make the decisions that you make" that it's not so much I'm making them, it's just that I'm leaning on God and praying that he can give me the kind of guidance I need.

BUCK WILLIAMS, FORMER NBA POWER FORWARD

Whatever was to my profit
I now consider loss for the sake of Christ.
What is more, I consider everything
a loss compared to the
surpassing greatness of knowing
Christ Jesus my Lord,
for whose sake I have lost all things.
I consider them rubbish,
that I may gain Christ.

PHILIPPIANS 3:7-8

*Hearing that Jesus had silenced the Sadducees, the
Pharisees got together. One of them, an expert in the law,
tested him with this question: "Teacher, which is the greatest
commandment in the Law?" Jesus replied: "'Love the Lord your God
with all your heart and with all your soul and with all your mind.'
This is the first and greatest commandment."*

MATTHEW 22:34-38

God, I want to become a champion, to fulfill my purpose in life. I admit that Jesus Christ is Your Son and that He promised to forgive me if I just ask. Forgive me for sinning, for compromising, for not pursuing a championship level in life. Wipe it out with your super weapon of forgiveness. Please clean my house and move in as Lord. I humble myself and admit that I need Your help to become a true champion in life. Please take me, change my life, and bring me into total victory. Thank You, Lord. Amen.

A.C. GREEN, NBA ALL STAR

*Jesus said, "So do not worry, saying, 'What shall we eat?'
or 'What shall we drink?' or 'What shall we wear?'
But seek first his kingdom and his righteousness, and
all these things will be given to you as well."*

MATTHEW 6:32-33

I've stumbled many times along the way and allowed my priorities to get out of line, but God has repeatedly shown me that I am to put nothing ahead of him in my life—not my wife, not my kids, not my ministry, and not my career. The more I'm able to put God first in all areas of my life, the more he's blessed me in them. I have a beautiful, loving wife, two great kids who are growing up to love the Lord, and a growing ministry as a player in the NFL. That has been the paradox of my putting God first in my life: The more I put my family, my ministry, and my career behind God on my list of priorities, the better those other areas have become.

When God is your top priority, that doesn't mean that you do it to the exclusion of those other areas of your life. When God is first in your life, those other areas take on a new, added importance simply because your heavenly Father is so interested in what you are doing. He wants to bless those other areas of your life simply because you glorify him when you succeed in your marriage, your career, and your ministry.

BRYCE PAUP, BUFFALO BILLS OUTSIDE LINEBACKER.

Prepare your minds for action; be self-controlled;
set your hope fully on the grace to be given you
when Jesus Christ is revealed.

1 PETER 1:13

9

Everybody Needs a Coach

For waging war you need guidance,
and for victory many advisers.

PROVERBS 24:6

A good coach provides the direction and concentration for performers' energies, helping channel all their efforts toward a single desired outcome. Without that critical influence, the best achievements of the most talented performers can lack the momentum and drive that make a group of individuals into champions.

I never set out to break George Halas's all-time coaching record of 324 wins. Naturally, I was proud when I surpassed it in the 1993 season, but the truth is, I never worry about win totals. They're a by-product of hard work of doing our best every day, every week, every year.

How long have I been coaching like this? Right from the beginning. From the moment I started coaching the Miami Dolphins in 1970, my day-to-day plan was very specific. I wanted to make sure we came out of every meeting a little more intelligent than when we went in, that we came off the practice field a little better prepared mentally and physically to play the game than we were before practice. I wanted us to make the most out of every meeting, every practice, and every preseason game to get us ready for the regular season.

DON SHULA, FORMER MIAMI DOLPHINS HEAD COACH

If you want to find a great coach, all you have to do is look at God's characteristics. All God cares about is the team. Yet in the same sense, all he cares about is the individual. Everything that happens in my life as a Christian is to make me a better team player and to make me a better person. Jesus is the best example of a teammate. He's the one who pats me on the back when I can't go any further. He's demanding, but loving. And when I fail, he sits me down and says, "Let's talk this over and try it again."

BRAD SMITH, FORMER COACH OF THE OREGON CITY PIONEERS
GIRLS BASKETBALL TEAM

*For we do not have a high priest who is unable to
sympathize with our weaknesses, but we have one who has been
tempted in every way, just as we are—yet was without sin.
Let us then approach the throne of grace with confidence,
so that we may receive mercy and find grace to
help us in our time of need.*

HEBREWS 4:15-16

I didn't realize when I first went to Nebraska that Coach Osborne was a Christian man. In fact, I didn't think it was possible for someone to be involved in football at that level and be a Christian. To me, it didn't look like there were many people involved in the game—players or coaches—who weren't cussing and carrying on like everybody else. I didn't know many players or coaches who professed to be Christians, at least not so everybody could hear it.

But as I got to know Tom and observed the way he carried himself, I saw there was something different in him. He didn't preach at us or try to convert us, but there was something about him that set him apart from the other people I knew. I still remember the first time somebody told me he was a strong Christian man. I thought, *That's right, he doesn't cuss.*

Coach Osborne had an influence on my life that has lasted to this day. He never wavered to the right or to the left, but was consistent in all his ways. If he said something, we could count on it.

Because Tom carried himself that way in front of us, we were that way as a team. I didn't understand it at the time, but now I look back and can see it. Without even thinking about it, we carried ourselves with the confidence and conviction that Tom Osborne had imparted to us.

IRVING FRYAR, FORMER PHILADELPHIA EAGLES WIDE RECEIVER

The Apostle Paul compares the Christian life to a race. Every Christian is called to run this race. It begins the moment we commit our lives to him, and it will conclude at the moment of death. Everything in life between these two moments is the race that God has set before us.

We must run God's race to win. We must press on to win the heavenly crown.

The essentials for winning the Christian race are much the same as those required to be a champion on the football field: self-discipline, determination, concentration, perseverance, dedication, and the will to win.

I know, because I sought to instill these qualities into the men whom I coached for almost thirty years with the Dallas Cowboys. These men became world champions. I also know these virtues are necessary in the Christian life. These are the character qualities that lead to victory in God's race—the race of faith.

TOM LANDRY, FORMER DALLAS COWBOYS COACH

Hold on to instruction, do not let it go;
guard it well, for it is your life.

PROVERBS 4:13

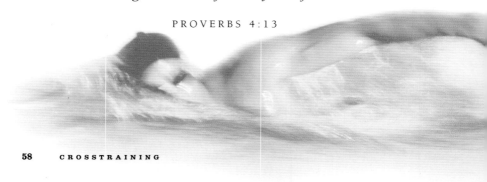

By the time you get to the pros, you've heard so many pep talks, you might think there's nothing left to listen to. But I found there was always *something* pertinent in what a coach had to say before a game, and I always listened for that. I wasn't looking for something to psyche me up. If you haven't already done that by the time you're about to take the field, it's too late.

DENNIS BYRD, FORMER NEW YORK JETS DEFENSIVE LINEMAN

He who scorns instruction will pay for it,
but he who respects a command is rewarded.

PROVERBS 13:13

You can tell a lot about a player by how he interacts with the coach. A player who argues with the coach over his decisions and then pouts at the far corner of the bench is clearly someone you don't want your daughter dating.

On the other hand, a player who listens to the coach, tries to do what he's told, and keeps the lines of communication open is a bonus for any team. An athlete like that picks up everyone's spirits, and this makes it much easier for the coach.

KEN RUETGGERS, FORMER GREEN BAY PACKER OFFENSIVE TACKLE

10

Go Team!

Be devoted to one another in brotherly love.
Honor one another above yourselves.

ROMANS 12:10

From day one in spring training, Scott Brosius began to get a sense his new team [the New York Yankees] was special. "Listening in the clubhouse, there was no talk at all about personal goals, like 'This is the year I'm going to hit thirty home runs,'" he says. "Everything was team-oriented. Our goal was to get to the playoffs and try to win a championship. The talent on the team goes without saying, but we also have a group of guys who are really special in their character."

Brosius soon found out many of his new teammates were Christians. Their season-long discipline of daily Bible study before games began during spring training. "So much of baseball is being comfortable where you are, and when you find some guys who share the same beliefs, who share the same thoughts that you do, when you have somebody to spend all that extra time with on the road, it makes the season go so much better," Brosius says.

Holmes, prayed and studied together at the ball park before batting practice. "I don't think we missed a day all year," Brosius says. A primary prayer for both the fellowship group and the team was for unity. Brosius believes the focus on team goals was God's answer. "For 25 guys to come together like that is rare," he says. "A lot of teams have the talent, but very seldom do they have the focus that this team had."

MIKE UMLANDT, WRITER FOR *SPORTS SPECTRUM* MAGAZINE

Two are better than one,
because they have a good return for their work:
If one falls down,
his friend can help him up.
But pity the man who falls
and has no one to help him up!
Though one may be overpowered,
two can defend themselves.
A cord of three strands is not quickly broken.

ECCLESIASTES 4:9,12

I appeal to you, brothers, in the name of our Lord Jesus Christ,
that all of you agree with one another so that
there may be no divisions among you and that you
may be perfectly united in mind and thought.

1 CORINTHIANS 1:10

Many superstars have an attitude of "Nobody is good enough to play with me." Or "I'm so much better than the rest of the team that I can be aloof." Julius [Erving] was just the opposite of that. He was the kind of guy who built his teammates up.

I remember one particular game when one of the players had two free-throws with three or four seconds to go. We had a chance to win the game if he would have made them. He missed them both. Julius was the first guy into the locker room. He went over beside the guy who missed the shots and said, "Hey, don't worry about it. We'll get it next time." He was an encourager. He was the kind of guy you like to have in your fox-hole, and I always appreciated that about Julius. He was there for you when you needed him.

BOBBY JONES, FORMER PHILADELPHIA 76ERS FORWARD

Encourage one another and build each other up,
just as in fact you are doing.

1 THESSALONIANS 5:11

I have always been very unabashed about how much I love the guys I played with, my coaches, and all the other people who are part of that family that makes up a team. These people mean so much to me.

DENNIS BYRD, FORMER NEW YORK JETS DEFENSIVE LINEMAN

Now the body is not made up of one part but of many. If the foot should say, "Because I am not a hand, I do not belong to the body," it would not for that reason cease to be part of the body. And if the ear should say, "Because I am not an eye, I do not belong to the body," it would not for that reason cease to be part of the body. If the whole body were an eye, where would the sense of hearing be? If the whole body were an ear, where would the sense of smell be? But in fact God has arranged the parts in the body, every one of them, just as he wanted them to be. If they were all one part, where would the body be? As it is, there are many parts, but one body. The eye cannot say to the hand, "I don't need you!" And the head cannot say to the feet, "I don't need you!" On the contrary, those parts of the body that seem to be weaker are indispensable, and the parts that we think are less honorable we treat with special honor. And the parts that are unpresentable are treated with special modesty, while our presentable parts need no special treatment. But God has combined the members of the body and has given greater honor to the parts that lacked it, so that there should be no division in the body, but that its parts should have equal concern for each other. If one part suffers, every part suffers with it; if one part is honored, every part rejoices with it.

1 CORINTHIANS 12:14-26

It was Jim Thome's birthday on a road trip in Anaheim. We all got together in the club house and decided that if we were going to make the playoffs we needed to start playing as a team. We had guys wanting to do their own thing all the time, so Seitz [Kevin Seitzer] stands up and tells everybody that we are going to play with high socks.

I know this sounds funny, but it really brought us together as a team. It took real humility for many of the players to wear high socks, including myself, because I flat-out didn't look good. But we were unified for a purpose, and it all started with the high socks.

MIKE JACKSON, CLEVELAND INDIANS RELIEF PITCHER

There was a real attitude of servanthood on our football team. Sixty guys kind of forgot about themselves, forgot about individual accolades, individual goals, and put the team ahead of themselves. To me, that was what was special. Everybody just kind of forgot about themselves and said, "I'm going to do whatever it takes to help our football team win." To me, that's what really brings the joy. We gave it up for one another, basically. That to me is very spiritual. That's about Christ. The Bible says that the Son of Man came to serve, not to be served. That was our whole football team last year.

MARK SCHLERETH, SUPER BOWL CHAMPION
DENVER BRONCOS OFFENSIVE GUARD

11

Butterflies

Be strong and courageous. Do not be afraid or terrified
because of them, for the LORD your God goes with you;
he will never leave you nor forsake you.

DEUTERONOMY 31:6

There's nothing like the nervousness that sweeps through you, the adrenaline rush that invades your body just before a kickoff. You know you can get blasted from anywhere, from any direction. Anyone who's ever played on a kickoff team knows the kind of butterflies I'm talking about.

My first college game was at home against Texas Tech. It was so scary going out there to run defensive plays. All I could see was what was directly in front of me. I was seized with tunnel vision, as if I had blinders on. I had no peripheral vision whatsoever. And that's dangerous. This is a game where peripheral vision is everything, where your sense of everything happening around you is crucial, where you're constantly soaking in and processing a flood of information, of visual cues: signals from the sidelines; keys from their players about what they're going to do; your strong linebacker barking out his calls while the quarterback's calling *his* signals; the defense changing and shifting. When you're young like that, there's so much information you *can't* absorb. You're dizzy trying to put everything together, your head is swimming from this cataclysmic overload. You're just about to snap from pressure, and then the ball's hiked, and then it all breaks loose. And all you've got to go on are your instincts.

DENNIS BYRD, FORMER NEW YORK JETS DEFENSIVE LINEMAN

My heart was racing, a hundred miles an hour. The noise was incredible. I looked at Terry and grabbed a bit of jersey over my heart, pounding it up and down to show him how my pulse was hammering. I pointed at him: "You too?" TK looked back and, with a big smile, signaled that his heart was doing the same thing.

Then I began to throw, just playing catch with Terry. As soon as I made the first toss, a sense of peace blanketed me. All I had to do now was what I know how to do best: throw a baseball.

DAVE DRAVECKY, FORMER SAN FRANCISCO GIANTS PITCHER

Do not be afraid. Stand firm and you will see the deliverance the LORD will bring you today.

EXODUS 14:13

It's April 3, 1994, and the NCAA championship is on the line. My team, the North Carolina Tar Heels, is battling the Louisiana Tech Techsters. We are down by two points, there's just seven-tenths of a second left—but we have possession. What would be our strategy?

In the huddle, coach Sylvia Hatchell, says, "We're going to go for the win and not the tie." But who's going to take the last shot? Who will be the chosen one? It would have to be someone who has perfected the three-point shot. There is no margin for error. Our minds are swirling as if we'd been swept up in a storm.

In order for UNC to win that game, there had to be someone appointed to take the last shot. Someone with faith and courage. Naturally, you would think Coach Hatchell would appoint the player who had perfected her three-point shot. Instead she decides to go with someone who's not even close to perfect.

During the storm of that title game, I was the player Coach Hatchell called on to take the last shot. I was shooting less than 25 percent for the season from behind the three-point line, but I accepted the challenge. As we walked out on the court for last possession, I quietly began to ask Jesus to grant me peace—and the ability to complete this task. I took the inbounds pass, put up the three-pointer, and it hit nothing but net. We had won North Carolina's first national championship in women's basketball.

CHARLOTTE SMITH, PLAYER FOR NORTH CAROLINA TAR HEELS

When you go to war against your enemies and see horses and
chariots and an army greater than yours, do not be afraid of them,
because the LORD your God, who brought you
up out of Egypt, will be with you.

DEUTERONOMY 20:1

Take up your positions; stand firm and see the deliverance
the LORD will give you, O Judah and Jerusalem.
Do not be afraid; do not be discouraged. Go out to face them
tomorrow, and the LORD will be with you.

2 CHRONICLES 20:17

We face pressures and struggles every day. But we have found a way to deal with them and live through them—with God's help—and you can, too. We can be on the path to victory, if we trust God with our lives.

JOHN SMOLTZ, ATLANTA BRAVES PITCHER

When I think of discipline, I think of our football team's off-season conditioning drills at Texas Tech. Our winter workouts (January, February, and March) prepared us for the fall football season (September, October, and November). The victories of the football season were often won months earlier in the winter training program. Any advantage we could achieve through conditioning our bodies would often mean the difference between victory and defeat.

STEVEN J. LAWSON, PASTOR AND AUTHOR OF *MEN WHO WIN*

See, the LORD your God has given you the land.
Go up and take possession of it as the LORD,
the God of your fathers, told you.
Do not be afraid; do not be discouraged.

DEUTERONOMY 1:21

As for being a Christian, the Bible speaks openly and frankly about competition in a healthy manner, about running the race in the manner in which you will win. That's the way I played football.

DENNIS BYRD, FORMER NEW YORK JETS DEFENSIVE LINEMAN

12

Game Day

When you are about to go into battle, the priest shall come forward and address the army. He shall say: "Hear, O Israel, today you are going into battle against your enemies; Do not be fainthearted or afraid; do not be terrified or give way to panic before them."

DEUTERONOMY 20:2-3

My Christian experience kept my boat anchored during my last three years in New Jersey. I had the privilege of being associated with a church called Redeeming Love Christian Center. And my faith really grew by leaps and bounds. A couple of verses in Romans that talk about how through adversity and hard times I should still be happy (Romans 5:3–4), helped me get through the whole ordeal . . . .

Everyone would always ask me, "Buck, how can you play so hard when you're not going to win any games?" But through it all, I knew deep in my heart that I was becoming a better person—I was building character. I was also becoming a better basketball player because I was playing on a losing team, which forced me to go out and do more things to help the team.

BUCK WILLIAMS, FORMER NBA POWER FORWARD

The thing that I'm very proud about is that I touched more lives through trials and tribulations—not getting any time in the playoffs, not getting any time during the course of the season. I touched more lives during that time than I did being Rookie of the Year and being an all-star, because, simply, I think a man is measured when his back is against the wall. How do you react? I responded by signing autographs, by going to the malls, still being the same person I've always been. And people were amazed by how positive I was, even though I was going through a struggle. But the main thing is, my trust wasn't in man, my trust was in God, and I thank God for those times.

MARK JACKSON, INDIANAPOLIS PACERS POINT GUARD

There's nothing like that feeling of sprinting out onto a football field at game time, emerging from the darkness of a stadium tunnel into the light of a Sunday afternoon, the sound of your echoing footsteps and the muted roar of the crowd replaced by the blast of 75,000 fans rocking the air you breathe. If you've got any fire in you at all, it's flaming by then.

DENNIS BYRD, FORMER NEW YORK JETS DEFENSIVE LINEMAN

The Jazz team is quite close. Thurl Bailey, the co-captain, is also a brother in Christ and he and Mark Eaton are best friends. Mark feels strongly that teamwork and a love for Christ are good ingredients in building a powerful pro basketball team. He says, "I think that being a Christian is a definite help when it comes to dedication and working hard on improving yourself. As a humble servant, I think I look at myself in the same terms. I'm never satisfied with my performance. I've never stopped working hard."

MARK LITTLETON, AUTHOR OF THE *SPORTS HEROES* BOOK SERIES

When the stadium's full, the crowd is yelling, and the referee raises his hand to signal the start of the game, I can feel the adrenaline rushing though my body. I wouldn't want to be anywhere else in the world. I think it's fabulous that I get paid for doing what I love to do.

DON SHULA, FORMER MIAMI DOLPHINS HEAD COACH

Be on your guard; stand firm in the faith;
be men of courage; be strong.

1 CORINTHIANS 16:13

I eagerly expect and hope that I will in no way be ashamed,
but will have sufficient courage so that now as always
Christ will be exalted in my body, whether by life or by death.
For to me, to live is Christ and to die is gain.

PHILIPPIANS 1:20-21

Act with courage, and may the LORD
be with those who do well.

2 CHRONICLES 19:11

Some trust in chariots and some in horses,
but we trust in the name of the LORD our God.
They are brought to their knees and fall,
but we rise up and stand firm.

PSALM 20:7-8

Halfway through the penalty kicks I looked at the scoreboard and saw we were tied 2-2. I knew it was my turn to do something for my country and my team. I prayed, "Lord, now is the time for me to defend against these penalty kicks. Please help me catch this one!"

The Lord granted my request. When Massaro kicked, I think God pushed me to the left side and I was able to stop the ball. Then Dunga scored for Brazil and we were down to the final kick.

After 52 games, 3 million tickets sold, 4 years of preparation, and a full month of world media, it all came down to Baggio and me. When I looked at him, I saw his head bent down with his eyes riveted to the ground. He appeared to me to be insecure and fearful. At that moment, I knew he was going to miss, or I would make the stop.

When he kicked the ball over the upper bar, the only thing that crossed my mind was to get down on my knees and give the glory to God. I knew the victory came from him alone, and I had to glorify him at that moment.

CLAUDIO TAFFAREL, GOALIE FOR BRAZIL'S
1994 WORLD CUP CHAMPIONS

Rise up; this matter is in your hands.
We will support you, so take courage and do it.

EZRA 10:4

13

A Good Sport

*Show proper respect
to everyone.*
1 PETER 2:17

've always been the kind of person who thrives on personal challenges. One of the most memorable was several years ago when I was still with the Patriots. Television analyst Cris Collinsworth, a pretty good receiver during his days with the Cincinnati Bengals, said during a broadcast that I was "washed up" and on my way out of the league. This was at the time when I was getting my life cleaned up after several years of the junk that everybody knew about.

The Bible tells me that I've got to forgive people when they say or do things against me, and I've forgiven Cris for what he said. It still motivates me to think that Collinsworth didn't think I could play anymore.

It was the same during the 1996 season. I saw what had been written about my age, and I heard the things people were saying. So I did what I've always done. I went out to prove them wrong.

I like to take on personal challenges and disprove people who doubt me.

That's always been a side of me that has helped me to excel during my football career.

IRVING FRYAR, FORMER PHILADELPHIA EAGLES WIDE RECEIVER

Respect is different from popularity. You can't make it happen or demand it from people. The only way you can get respect is to earn it.

DON SHULA, FORMER MIAMI DOLPHINS HEAD COACH

Always be prepared to give an answer to everyone who asks you to give the reason for the hope that you have. But do this with gentleness and respect, keeping a clear conscience.

1 PETER 3:15–16

Each of you should look not only to your own interests, but also to the interests of others.

PHILIPPIANS 2:4

*All who are under the yoke of slavery should
consider their masters worthy of full respect, so that
God's name and our teaching may not be slandered. Those who
have believing masters are not to show less respect for them because
they are brothers. Instead, they are to serve them even better,
because those who benefit from their service are believers,
and dear to them. These are the things you are
to teach and urge on them.*

1 TIMOTHY 6:1-2

The relationship I want to establish with my football team is one of mutual respect. I want my players to respect me for giving them everything that I have to prepare them to play the best that they can play. My respect for them has to come from knowing that they are willing to give me all that they have to prepare themselves to be ready to play.

DON SHULA, FORMER MIAMI DOLPHINS HEAD COACH

Give everyone what you owe him: If you owe taxes,
pay taxes; if revenue, then revenue; if respect, then respect;
if honor, then honor. Let no debt remain outstanding, except the
continuing debt to love one another, for he who loves his fellowman
has fulfilled the law. The commandments, "Do not commit adultery,"
"Do not murder," "Do not steal," "Do not covet," and whatever other
commandment there may be, are summed up in this one rule:
"Love your neighbor as yourself." Love does no harm to its neighbor.
Therefore love is the fulfillment of the law.

ROMANS 13:7-10

As important as it is for athletes to respect authority on the
playing field, the feeling should be mutual when it comes to coaches
respecting players.

REV. HENRY SOLES, CHAPLAIN FOR THE CHICAGO BULLS

Just as each of us has one body with many members,
and these members do not all have the same function, so
in Christ we who are many form one body, and each member
belongs to all the others. We have different gifts,
according to the grace given us.

ROMANS 12:4-6

For a long time, soccer was it for me. It was my God. I believed I could make all my money playing soccer. When I got saved, it changed my whole perspective on soccer and life. With God, I had a direction. I wanted to serve him. Now with the platform he's given me, I can really see how he's leading. My life is a testimony to others. People will pay attention to soccer, and through soccer to a Christian testimony.

DESMOND ARMSTRONG, SOCCER DEFENDER AND SWEEPER

My faith insists that we are all equal in the eyes of God. And football nurtures intimacy and brotherhood. Nothing can bring a group of individuals closer together than to see one another bleed and sweat, laugh and cry, win and lose. Once you've been through war with a man, race becomes a trivial thing. They had a saying in Vietnam, where black and white U.S. troops fought together for the first time as fully integrated units: Same mud, same blood. That's how it is with football, too.

DENNIS BYRD, FORMER NEW YORK JETS DEFENSIVE LINEMAN

Now we ask you, brothers, to respect those who work hard among you, who are over you in the Lord and who admonish you. Hold them in the highest regard in love because of their work.

1 THESSALONIANS 5:12–13

14

Time Out

Jesus said, "Come with me by yourselves
to a quiet place and get some rest."

MARK 6:31

Anybody who's familiar with the human body knows that it is indeed possible to over train, to push your body beyond the limits of what it was intended to take. When that happens, you become a victim of the law of diminishing returns—the more you do, the less benefit you get. If you continue, you eventually do more harm than good in your workouts. That's exactly what happened to me.

I figured that to stay on top I had to refine my body. So I found a physical therapist and worked throughout the off-season. I worked and worked and worked, driving one hour each way three times a week in the process. I became obsessed with working out. I worked on parts of my body that had given me problems during my NFL career, I worked on my steps, and I worked on things that I'd never even thought of working on before. It got to the point where it seemed like I needed fifty hours a week to get everything done. . . .

Instead of getting physically better that off-season, I got worse. I burned myself out and just spun my wheels in my training. I was physically and emotionally exhausted, but I couldn't take the time to recharge my batteries because I was trying so hard to improve and meet the needs and desires of other people.

I was burning out spiritually, but I couldn't see it at the time. I believed I was doing the right thing, because I'd always been taught that God honors hard work. I thought I was doing what I needed to do to glorify him. Eventually, though, God gave me a message I couldn't help but hear: Slow down!

BRYCE PAUP, BUFFALO BILLS OUTSIDE LINEBACKER

One thing our staff holds in high regard is what God says about the Sabbath. A lot of Division 1 coaches don't take a day off during their season, but we really feel that we want to respond to God's Word and obey that principle of resting one day a week. Each one of us takes a day off where we just do not do basketball. I really feel that's been an enhancement to the balance we have in our lives. It's amazing what God will do in the other 6 days when you honor him.

SUE SEMRAU, FLORIDA STATE WOMEN'S BASKETBALL HEAD COACH

Six days do your work, but on the seventh day do not work, so that your ox and your donkey may rest and the slave born in your household, and the alien as well, may be refreshed.

EXODUS 23:12

Now Ahab told Jezebel everything Elijah had done and how he had killed all the prophets with the sword. So Jezebel sent a messenger to Elijah to say, "May the gods deal with me, be it ever so severely, if by this time tomorrow I do not make your life like that of one of them." Elijah was afraid and ran for his life. When he came to Beersheba in Judah, he left his servant there, while he himself went a day's journey into the desert. He came to a broom tree, sat down under it and prayed that he might die. "I have had enough, LORD," he said. "Take my life; I am no better than my ancestors." Then he lay down under the tree and fell asleep. All at once an angel touched him and said, "Get up and eat." He looked around, and there by his head was a cake of bread baked over hot coals, and a jar of water. He ate and drank and then lay down again. The angel of the LORD came back a second time and touched him and said, "Get up and eat, for the journey is too much for you." So he got up and ate and drank. Strengthened by that food, he traveled forty days and forty nights until he reached Horeb, the mountain of God.

1 KINGS 19:1-8

The end of Day 20 brought more than the promise of another night's sleep. We were exhausted by this point in our trip—in large measure because we hadn't yet taken a full day off—and the wear and tear was beginning to show. For the last several days Brian had been complaining about pain in the back of his knee. Despite taking several ibuprofen tablets each morning before beginning to ride, his leg began to throb after a few hours. I wasn't having any knee problems, but I sure needed the rest. I felt as if I'd been up several nights in a row, cramming for exams. Every fiber in my body was exhausted.

In my first radio job, I worked the overnight shift and had a hard time sleeping during the day. I would catch up on the weekends, but by Wednesday I was wrung out. I can remember driving home in the morning rush hour traffic, slapping myself to stay awake. More times than I want to recall, while behind the wheel I would jerk to an awareness that I didn't remember the last several miles. I must have been in some presleep stupor. I'm amazed I never had an accident.

I was fast approaching that same level of fatigue as we pushed on toward Virginia Beach, Virginia, and I knew it wasn't good. That's why we had scheduled two days off. Brian would use most of that time to return to Colorado Springs to attend his brother's high school graduation while I would rest, work on our bikes, do laundry, and enjoy the company of my hosts.

MIKE TROUT, CO-HOST OF THE FOCUS ON THE FAMILY RADIO PRO-
GRAM, ON HIS CROSS-COUNTRY BICYCLE TRIP

Eric Liddell made headlines all over the world in 1924 when he refused to compete in his strongest event, the 100 meters, because the qualifying heats were held on Sunday. Liddell, the son of Scottish missionaries, was a deeply committed Christian. Like many Christians in his day, he believed that Sunday should be set aside for worship, not worldly pursuits or pleasures. His stand brought him criticism and ridicule. When he refused to yield to the pressure brought to bear by the British government and the Olympic committee, he was described as fanatical and uncooperative.

Yet Liddell was prepared to sacrifice everything for which he had worked, all of his athletic dreams and goals, for the sake of his moral principles and spiritual convictions.

When officials couldn't convince him to run the 100 meters on Sunday, Britain's Olympic committee entered him in a different race. In true storybook finish, Liddell won two Olympic medals, the bronze in the 200 meters and the gold in the 400 meters—and he set an Olympic record in the process.

CHRISTIN DITCHFIELD, WRITER FOR *SPORTS SPECTRUM* MAGAZINE

Jesus said, "Come to me, all you who are weary and burdened, and I will give you rest. Take my yoke upon you and learn from me, for I am gentle and humble in heart, and you will find rest for your souls. For my yoke is easy and my burden is light."

MATTHEW 11:28-30

15

Bouncing Back

We are hard pressed on every side, but not crushed; perplexed,
but not in despair; persecuted, but not abandoned;
struck down, but not destroyed.

2 CORINTHIANS 4:8–9

I got to witness firsthand Don Shula's capacity to rebound from a setback, in December 1994 when the Dolphins were blown off the field in the second half of a disappointing 42-31 Sunday-night loss to the Buffalo Bills. The Dolphins were 8-4 at the time, and a win over their archrival would insure them a play-off berth and eliminate the perennial Super Bowl contenders. The Dolphins were leading 17-7 at half-time, and then the roof caved in. I was part of a group that waited in the Shula sky box for Don to appear after the game. When he did, he looked completely drained and exhausted. A friend tried to give him encouragement by saying, "Don't worry, Don, you'll get them next time. I know we'll make the play-offs."

Don was quick to intervene. "What I don't need right now is a pep talk."

Shula needed the space to feel the loss deeply so he could then focus his, the coaches', and the team's energy on the next opponent, Kansas City.

When I saw Don on Monday night before his weekly TV show, he was a different person. His mind was already on Kansas City. While he reviewed the Buffalo game on his show, you could see the hurt was over. As we ate dinner and watched the Raiders beat the Chargers, Don Shula had already left the loss behind and was preparing for the next battle. And I'm sure his team was, too, especially the way they blew Kansas City out of the water, 45-21, the following Monday night. After the game, in typical Shula fashion, Don told the press, "We've clinched it. Now we're looking toward these next two games and the best possible situation we can have in the play-offs."

KEN BLANCHARD, AUTHOR OF *EVERYONE'S A COACH*

> *It is God who arms me with strength*
> *   and makes my way perfect.*
> *He makes my feet like the feet of a deer;*
> *   he enables me to stand on the heights.*
> *He trains my hands for battle;*
> *   my arms can bend a bow of bronze.*
> *You give me your shield of victory,*
> *   and your right hand sustains me;*
> *   you stoop down to make me great.*
> *You broaden the path beneath me,*
> *   so that my ankles do not turn.*

PSALM 18:32-36

We came home for our first game in Skelly Stadium, and it was one the whole state had been looking forward to: Oklahoma. It had been forty-five years since the Sooners last played in Tulsa. More than 47,000 people squeezed into Skelly (six thousand more than there were seats) to see us play our third top-ranked opponent in four years.

What they saw was a nightmare (ours).

Oklahoma scored nine touchdowns and a field goal. We scored nothing. Jamelle Holieway took the afternoon off early, and his replacement, Charles Thompson, ran for three touchdowns and 105 yards on *eight* carries. Lydell Carr, my teammate from the high school All-State game, didn't have a bad afternoon either. He had a sweet little thirty-five yard dash in the second quarter that made the half-time score 31-0. They ended up shellacking us 65-zip.

It's humiliating to lose by scores like that. It hurts. But I believe that's the kind of thing that tempers you as a person, that teaches you to see what you've really got inside you. All that losing did was make my resolve even stronger. The way I felt was that we had sixty minutes of football to play every Saturday, and if we were down by sixty points and it was only the beginning of the third quarter, we still owed somebody thirty more minutes. I couldn't imagine not giving everything I had every second I was on that field. No matter what the score, no matter whether it was the first play of the game or the last, I always took it personally. I considered each play a game in itself, and I got very upset if I ever saw anybody beside me giving up even a little bit.

DENNIS BYRD, FORMER NEW YORK JETS DEFENSIVE LINEMAN

If the other team scores, forget about it as soon as it happens. Go on to the next one. Always think of making a shutout. You have to be the first one to pick the ball up out of the goal. You have to send a message to your team, "That's it. No more."

PAUL ZIMMERMAN, SOCCER GOALIE

Jesus said, "Now get up and stand on your feet."

ACTS 26:16

*We are not of those who shrink back and are destroyed,
but of those who believe and are saved.*

HEBREWS 10:39

God didn't say, "David, we're going to make you lose in the play-offs and we're going to make Hakeem Olajuwon play great so you'll look like a clown." He didn't say that to hurt my feelings, and he wasn't trying to hurt my feelings. He was trying to say, "David, you need to mature. You need to get stronger. You need to get better. So you can either cry about it or you can get better."

Failure doesn't get enough credit. It teaches us humility, perseverance, and the value of hard work. When you fail, you have to learn from your mistakes and move on. God gives you challenges in your life, but he gives them to you for a reason. It's not like he's trying to hurt you or punish you. He's giving you those challenges so you'll grow up and mature.

DAVID ROBINSON, SAN ANTONIO SPURS CENTER

That's the miracle. That's the magic. It's knowing that all of life is a blessing, that the Lord is with us even if we falter, He is with us even if we fail, He is with us when we break, and He can help to make us whole.

I've always believed that.

And I always will.

DENNIS BYRD, FORMER NEW YORK JETS DEFENSIVE LINEMAN

16

Staying the Course

*Let us run with perseverance
the race marked out for us.*
HEBREWS 12:1

I learned right away that nothing comes easy in this game. The pre-season two-a-days at Mustang were as tough as any I would ever go through in all my years of football. For two weeks we were out there in the broiling Oklahoma sun, the grass just cut, our skin hot and itching as we did hours and hours of monkey rolls, calisthenics, and wind sprints in the morning and again in the afternoon. I'd never been through anything like it. At one point I turned to my brother Dan and said, "Man, I don't want to *do* this." He and Doug were in my face in a heartbeat.

"Excuse me?" they said. "If you quit now, we're gonna kick your butt."

And they would have, badly. My brothers wouldn't let anyone else lay a hand on me, but they were allowed to beat the stuffing out of me at will.

So I endured. And a whole world was opened up to me, a world I hadn't really understood until then.

DENNIS BYRD, FORMER NEW YORK JETS DEFENSIVE LINEMAN

We pray this in order that you may live a life worthy
of the Lord and may please him in every way: bearing fruit
in every good work, growing in the knowledge of God, being
strengthened with all power according to his glorious might so that
you may have great endurance and patience, and joyfully giving
thanks to the Father, who has qualified you to share in the
inheritance of the saints in the kingdom of light.

COLOSSIANS 1:10-12

We do not want you to be uninformed, brothers, about
the hardships we suffered in the province of Asia. We were
under great pressure, far beyond our ability to endure, so that we
despaired even of life. Indeed, in our hearts we felt the sentence of
death. But this happened that we might not rely on ourselves
but on God, who raises the dead. He has delivered us from
such a deadly peril, and he will deliver us. On him we
have set our hope that he will continue to deliver us.

2 CORINTHIANS 1:8-10

If the other team scores, forget about it as soon as it happens. Go on to the next one. . . . If you commit a sin, confess it and forget it, then go on.

PAUL ZIMMERMAN, CHARLOTTE EAGLES

When it's the fourth quarter and you're behind, *way* behind, and you're a defensive lineman making a tackle downfield, beating a defensive back to the ball, and you come up off the bottom of that pile because you got there first, you don't have to say a whole lot. You've challenged the other guys. You've said, "Hey. Look. There's still a game going on. There's still a reason to play hard."

DENNIS BYRD, FORMER NEW YORK JETS DEFENSIVE LINEMAN

You know that the testing of your faith develops perseverance.
Perseverance must finish its work so that you may be
mature and complete, not lacking anything.

JAMES 1:3–4

Perseverance would definitely describe me, with faith in parentheses. Because I've had to persevere through a lot of different things on and off the court. And I've had to walk by faith and not by sight in a lot of situations.

AVERY JOHNSON, SAN ANTONIO SPURS POINT GUARD

First, there was the *weight-lifting room*. This was designed to build our bodily strength. To make us strong. Specially designed weight machines could accommodate three or four athletes, each working on a separate exercise. The athletes advanced through the weight room, pumping the weights as many times as they could. We moved from one machine to the next, like a long train winding through a valley. This was all designed to build up our muscles. Every exercise had specific muscles it was designed to bulk up and strengthen. No muscle was overlooked or left dormant.

Second, there was the *agility room*. This was designed to develop body control, coordination, agility, and quickness. In a fast and furious fifteen minutes, athletes would run in place, roll sideways, and somersault backward and forward, all to the response of a coach's signal. We were able to do things with our body that we never dreamed possible.

The third workout station was the *wind sprints*. These were fun on the football field itself and were designed to develop our speed and quickness. We would line up and run fifty-yard wind sprints at a coach's signal. We would have about thirty seconds to catch our breath. Then another coach would signal us to sprint back to the first coach. This would be repeated quickly for the entire fifteen-minute period.

The fourth workout station was *running the stadium bleachers*. Running the long climb to the top of the stadium and then back down was the chosen method of self-inflicted torture. The purpose was to build up our stamina, endurance, and perseverance, not to mention our character. We were ready to die, but we kept pressing on. We couldn't just quit.

STEVEN J. LAWSON, PASTOR AND AUTHOR OF *MEN WHO WIN*

We face pressures and struggles every day. But we have found a way to deal with them and live through them with God's help, and you can too. We can be on the path to victory, if we trust God with our lives.

JOHN SMOLTZ, ATLANTA BRAVES PITCHER

The master in the art of living makes little distinction between his work and his play, his labor and his leisure, his mind and his body, his information and his recreation, his love and his religion. He hardly knows which is which. He simply pursues his vision of excellence at whatever he does, leaving others to decide whether he is working or playing. To him he's always doing both.

JAMES MICHENER

I had my athletic and physical training to thank for my recovery. That helped enormously in terms of understanding what pain is, what effort and determination are, what it means to push and push and, when you feel like collapsing, to push some more. Never give up. I'd learned that lesson on the football field.

DENNIS BYRD, FORMER NEW YORK JETS DEFENSIVE LINEMAN

17

A Winning Attitude

*Finally, brothers, whatever is true, whatever is noble,
whatever is right, whatever is pure, whatever is lovely,
whatever is admirable—if anything is excellent or
praiseworthy—think about such things.*

PHILIPPIANS 4:8

To be successful in the major leagues you need to stay focused on your job. One of the things about being a Christian is that you have the ultimate guidance counselor, so your focus is on one thing and not everything else around you. You have a goal in mind, and with God's help, all you have to do is apply yourself toward that goal. It's the same way with baseball. My game has really benefited from the fact that I became a Christian. That's when everything came together for me. I went from a scatterbrained young kid to a pitcher who realized that there was a purpose to facing a particular hitter. It's very much the same way in the game of life. You have to take it seriously and you have to set goals for yourself.

JOHN WETTELAND, TEXAS RANGERS PITCHER

Let's go back in time to the 1950s. Ted Williams was in the batting cage at Boston's Fenway Park taking his cuts. Unequivocally, the "Splendid Splinter" is one of the greatest hitters of all time. Arguably, the purest hitter in the game's history. Williams remains baseball's last .400 hitter, and when Ted called it quits, he retired with 521 lifetime home runs and a .344 career batting average.

What made Ted such a great hitter? Great eyesight? Perfect hand-eye coordination? Being a student of hitting? Yes, all of these things, but most of all, a rare ability to concentrate on the pitch. To block out all distractions. To focus.

As the story goes, his Red Sox teammates decided to test his notorious concentration skills by playing a prank on Williams. While Ted was hitting in the batting cage, his teammates quietly lit some firecrackers and tossed them at his feet.

Boom! Boom! Boom!

Guess what? Ted was so focused, he did not even blink. As the firecrackers went off at his feet, his eyes remained riveted on the pitch. He was so intense that he could block out every distraction. Even exploding firecrackers.

Winners must be focused. Like Ted Williams.

STEVEN J. LAWSON, PASTOR AND AUTHOR OF *MEN WHO WIN*

You need Jesus Christ as your focal point. For example, everything else around you changes—like I had to change in my life from New Jersey to Portland. I had another change in my life when I had my son. In other words, as everything around you changes, you keep your focus on the Lord, as the Bible talks about, "seek ye first the kingdom of God . . . and these things will be added to you" (Matthew 6:33, KJV).

And that's my way of thinking. Seeking the kingdom of God keeps me focused—which is so important in my life and so important when I walk out on the floor. I need to be focused on what I have to get done while everything else around me is changing. It could be a change in our defense, or the other team may put in a different player to guard me, or the pace of the game may change. But if I can stay focused on what has to be done in terms of rebounding and playing defense, I will be more consistent, and I will get the reward in the end.

BUCK WILLIAMS, FORMER NBA POWER FORWARD

Your attitude should be the same as that of Christ Jesus:
who made himself nothing, taking the very nature of a servant,
being made in human likeness.

PHILIPPIANS 2:5-7

God has been a big part of my life and my family's life. We've relied on him to guide our lives in every facet that's come about—whether it be a career change or sickness or where are we going to be next year. The best part of the whole thing is the fact that once I've given the decision to the Lord to make, I don't worry about it. That's one thing I've always been good at. I don't get too stressed out about decisions. I just say, Lord, help me with this. I'm going to give it to you—like that verse that says, don't worry about anything. The whole basis of my life is that I don't get stressed about things I don't have control over.

MARK EATON, FORMER UTAH JAZZ CENTER

In a controlled scrimmage the teams don't keep track of downs or touchdowns but simply run plays to see how certain defenses work against certain offenses and vice versa.

An hour and a half into the scrimmage, the Eagles' defense lined up against the Lions' offense. Reggie White had outplayed and outmaneuvered the rookie offensive player across from him on the line. But during one play their helmets got locked together. It was one of those moments when everybody has to show how tough they are. The rookie sounded off—with some of the worst language Reggie had ever heard. It's not that Reggie's not used to bad language—you hear it in football (even though no one has ever heard him swear himself)—but this was a stream of filth unlike any other.

When the rookie got done spouting his garbage, Reggie pointed a finger at his nose and said, "Jesus is coming back soon, and I hope you're ready!"

The rookie (and everyone else) was so stunned, he looked in shock. Then he fired back more choice words at Reggie.

Standing there, livid with rage, Reggie refused to return to his huddle. He shouted across the field, "Jesus is coming back soon, and I hope you're ready."

Some teammates pressed Reggie to get back in the huddle. But he only moved into his position on the line of scrimmage, then shouted, "Jesus is coming back soon, and I hope he's ready."

The whole field went deathly quiet. And Reggie shouted one more time, "Jesus is coming back soon, and I don't think you're ready."

Finally, the Lions broke their huddle and Reggie lined up in position against this rookie. He seethed once more, "Jesus is coming back soon, and *I don't think you're ready.*"

Reggie listened as the quarterback called signals. The ball was snapped. He locked eyes with the rookie and declared, "Here comes Jesus!"

He pounced, hustled the rookie back about five yards, then knocked him onto his rear end. A second later, Reggie sacked the QB.

Everyone on the Eagles loved this play so much that for years afterward they would joke, "Is Jesus coming back on the next play, Reg?"

MARK LITTLETON, AUTHOR OF THE *SPORTS HEROES* BOOK SERIES

18

Going for the Gold

Do your best to present yourself to God as one approved,
a workman who does not need to be ashamed.

2 TIMOTHY 2:15

What has produced winning football teams for us over the years has been our willingness to create practice systems and procedures that are aligned with our vision of perfection: *We want to win them all.* Everything I do is to prepare people to perform to the best of their ability. And you do that one day at a time.

I believe that if you don't seek perfection, you can never reach excellence. Maybe it was because I regarded an unbeaten NFL season as a possibility that the feat became a reality. In 1972 the Miami Dolphins won every game, including the Super Bowl. That was the thrill of a lifetime. You may ask, "How can you do any better than that? How can you be better than perfection?" Well, you can't. But it certainly has set a standard that no one will forget and one toward which I want my teams to always strive.

DON SHULA, FORMER MIAMI DOLPHIN HEAD COACH

The quality of a man's life is in direct proportion to his commitment to excellence.

Those who have trusted in God [must] be careful to devote themselves to doing what is good. These things are excellent and profitable for everyone.

TITUS 3:8

I have a responsibility to put it out on the floor every night and be the best I can be. This is the way I minister to people right now. People have watched me grow and change over the years. They've seen the difference in the way I've focused on the game and become more dedicated.

DAVID ROBINSON, SAN ANTONIO SPURS CENTER

As a result of my searching I became very passionate. I took on anything, was engulfed in it 100 percent, good, bad, or indifferent. All that did was form a foundation of absolute confusion. It was like trying to search for something you needed and you knew was out there, but no one was telling you where it was. If you talk with anyone who filled their life with the things I did, he will tell you he had unfulfilled peace. Easter cults, philosophy, psychology, I read everything.

I was conscious only of the fact that I was missing something, and the something I was missing was big. I kept turning from one thing to another.

Finally I started realizing, "I need that peace; everything I've been living for is wrong." I got on my knees and wept.

JOHN WETTELAND, TEXAS RANGERS PITCHER

I believe in being the best I can be at whatever I do. I continually evaluate who I am and what my life is about to make sure I am being the best I can be. Yet I have come to realize that it takes time to grow up, no matter how old you are—and I'm still growing up. I'm learning that I can endure this journey and the ongoing struggles best when I accept that I am a man who has faults and a man who is still in the process of learning and growing toward maturity. Life is more manageable when I realize it calls for one comeback after another.

DAVE DRAVECKY, FORMER SAN FRANCISCO GIANTS PITCHER

The Northern Iowa defensive coordinator, Pete Rodriguez, gave me the kind of incentive I needed to get me through those first few weeks of fall football practice. Just a few days after I had told Denise I didn't know if I belonged here, he took me aside and said, "Bryce, if you keep working at it, you could become one of the best linemen in this college's history."

I don't know if Pete knew what I was going through at the time, or if he had simply seen enough college freshmen to know that they needed a pat on the back like that to keep them going. I do know this: God knew that I needed encouragement, and Coach Rodriguez's words were just what I needed to hear, when I needed to hear them. After that talk with the coach, I started to believe that I belonged at Northern Iowa.

BRYCE PAUP, BUFFALO BILLS ALL-PRO OUTSIDE LINEBACKER

How could a quiet, mild-mannered person pillage and plunder on the field? I don't have any single answer, only the knowledge that when I step on the field I'm playing for the glory of God and I won't settle for second best . . . . God gave me the ability to play, and my gift to him is what I do with it.

MIKE SINGLETARY, FORMER ALL-PRO MIDDLE LINEBACKER FOR THE CHICAGO BEARS

No matter what you do, just put God first. Be strongly committed to him, because without him we are nothing. And I don't want Jesus to think that what he did on the cross was in vain for me. I want to continue to do all that I can while I'm on this journey. That's pretty much what I try to share with kids: putting God first and just striving for excellence.

God sent his best gift in Jesus, so whenever you're in the classroom or whenever you're participating in sports or whatever it is, do it to the best of your ability.

AVERY JOHNSON, SAN ANTONIO SPURS POINT GUARD

If Jesus were in my shoes, called to compete as a professional athlete, he would be the best athlete on the field. He would play with more intensity and aggressiveness than any other athlete. But he would always be under control.

Whatever Jesus did, whether preaching to crowds or caring for a single, insignificant individual, he did it uncompromisingly, intensely, and powerfully. As anybody who has read the Bible knows, Jesus was no wimp. So if I imagine Jesus doing the job I'm called to do, I can easily imagine him doing it in a way I would have to respect.

DAVE DRAVECKY, FORMER SAN FRANCISCO GIANTS PITCHER

Serve wholeheartedly, as if you were serving the Lord, not men, because you know that the Lord will reward everyone for whatever good he does, whether he is slave or free.

EPHESIANS 6:7-8

19

The Thrill of Victory

When the righteous triumph,
there is great elation.
PROVERBS 28:12

I t was bad weather that day. Raining. Windy. Cold. We were playing at St. John Fisher College in Rochester, New York. Before the game I actually felt sick, a little flu or something. It wasn't until late in the second half that I really started to come on and feel better. The first two goals I hardly remember. They passed by in a blur because I felt so sick. We were ranked pretty high in the country at the time. In the top ten. It was a big game for us. Their players were loud, yelling, swearing, nasty. Calling us wimps and stuff like that. The crowd was yelling at us, too. They said we were nothing in the rain, and individually we didn't have any talent—in so many words, if you get my meaning.

I remember hitting the crossbar a few times. I kicked at the goal probably eight or nine times that day.

Then in the second half with ten minutes to go, I remember getting the ball out in front of the bench and hearing from the sidelines, "He is nothing. He's no one. Take the ball away from him." I wanted to prove something, even though I'd already scored two goals. So I gritted my teeth and dribbled down toward their goal. On the way, beat a few defenders, then shot. We scored. That calmed the crowd down a bit. People were double-teaming me, but I wasn't really thinking about it.

My fourth goal that day was similar to the third. I took the ball about forty yards from the goal. Beat a couple defenders. Shot at around ten yards. Goalie was coming out. The ball ripped past him. A piece of cake.

My fifth goal was a penalty kick. The crowd was really screaming now. But I stood at the line and the goalie looked at me like, *I'm not gonna let you beat me this time.* I figured I'd go for one side or the other. Ran up. Swatted it. The goalkeeper leaped to his left. But I kicked it to his right. It went in. Game over, 5-1.

JAMES WELLINGTON, SOCCER FORWARD

It [winning the World Series] was everything I imagined. Days and weeks and months from now, I'm sure it will grow deeper in meaning. But right now I'm very peaceful with it. Yes, you get excited, and there's a rush of adrenaline. But there's something very peaceful about it.

PAUL MOLITOR, FORMER TORONTO BLUE JAYS FIRST BASEMAN

The *San Francisco Chronicle* wrote of my pitching that day [in game two of the 1987 National League pennant game], "It was so easy it seemed effortless. It was so effortless it seemed boring." Perhaps so, but not to me. I was pitching the game of my life. Every time the 55,331 fans stirred to life, I quieted them. There on the mound, throwing my pitches, I was able to completely control the mood and the tempo of the game. It was an incredible feeling of power.

DAVE DRAVECKY, FORMER SAN FRANCISCO GIANTS PITCHER

He will yet fill your mouth with laughter
and your lips with shouts of joy.

JOB 8:21

This is love for God: to obey his commands.
And his commands are not burdensome, for everyone
born of God overcomes the world. This is the victory that
has overcome the world, even our faith.

1 JOHN 5:3-4

Boy, did I feel good. I wasn't a member of the walking wounded any longer. I was a pitcher, playing the only way I know how: all out, nothing held back. I'd gotten my uniform dirty.

I don't even remember how I got the last out. I just remember all the players congregating on the mound, slapping me and yelling as though we had won a playoff game. The crowd was yelling, too.

The truth is, when I search through my baseball memories, I don't find any game happier than that one. I was on top of the world.

DAVE DRAVECKY, FORMER SAN FRANCISCO GIANTS PITCHER

May the God of hope fill you with all joy and peace
as you trust in him, so that you may overflow with hope
by the power of the Holy Spirit.

ROMANS 15:13

Thanks be to God! He gives us the victory
through our Lord Jesus Christ.

1 CORINTHIANS 15:57

These are men whose burning passion is winning. At any cost. So they remove all encumbrances that would hinder a swift performance.

Just as the first-century athletes stripped down to run with maximum speed, we must strip away every spiritual encumbrance that would impede our progress in God's race. Pursuing the ultimate prize requires laying aside anything that would slow us down.

Hebrews 12:1 says, "Therefore, since we have so great a cloud of witnesses surrounding us, *let us also lay aside every encumbrance*" (emphasis added). This is a call for "spiritual streaking."

Too many of us run as if outfitted with layers of restrictive clothing and with heavy weights. We must strip down and run unencumbered. Take it all off!

STEVEN J. LAWSON, PASTOR AND AUTHOR OF *MEN WHO WIN*

For the LORD gives wisdom,and
from his mouth come knowledge and understanding.
He holds victory in store for the upright,
he is a shield to those whose walk is blameless.

PROVERBS 2:6-7

20

Keeping Your
Eye on the Goal

*Our citizenship is in heaven. And we eagerly await a Savior
from there, the Lord Jesus Christ, who, by the power that enables
him to bring everything under his control, will transform our
lowly bodies so that they will be like his glorious body.*

PHILIPPIANS 3:20-21

Has anyone ever "fixed you with a stare"? If so, you know it's not just any old look. It's not a glance. It's not a casual observation. It's not a nod in your direction to acknowledge your presence. It's an eye lock, a deliberate and prolonged gaze that shuts out every other possible focus of attention. It's as if a shaft of carbon steel has been welded from another person's eyes to yours.

In much that way, I used to lock on my catcher's glove when I was pitching in the major leagues. Batters were merely distractions, especially if they were good hitters. My goal was to so focus on my catcher's glove that I wouldn't even see the batter.

It is this kind of stare we are instructed to level at the unseen things of God. Countless distractions will clamor for our attention, trying feverishly to seduce our eyes to drift in their direction, but God urges us to fix our gaze on his eternal truths. Only in that way will we be enabled to look past the vicious cuts life takes at us and wind up with a big "W" on our final scoreboard.

DAVE DRAVECKY, FORMER SAN FRANCISCO GIANT PITCHER

It makes a real difference to me when I start off each day by giving thanks and asking for help from God. Belief in something bigger than you is important. People close to me will tell you I'm not a real pleasant person after losing a football game, but I'd be a lot worse if I didn't realize that something far bigger than football exists. There's something good about kneeling down, asking for help, and listening for answers.

DON SHULA, FORMER MIAMI DOLPHIN HEAD COACH

In recent years, Don has gotten a lot of assistance from two players who help keep winning and losing in perspective. If we've lost a game, and the team gets on the plane in really low spirits, two deeply spiritual players go around helping people get up off the ground and come back to prepare for the next game. They also never get too excited when we win. If the players are sky-high after a victory, these guys also help calm things down so we're in mental shape for the next game.

MARY ANNE SHULA, WIFE OF COACH DON SHULA

Since we are surrounded by such a great cloud of witnesses,
let us throw off everything that hinders and the sin that so easily
entangles, and let us run with perseverance the race marked out
for us. Let us fix our eyes on Jesus, the author and perfecter of our
faith, who for the joy set before him endured the cross, scorning its
shame, and sat down at the right hand of the throne of God.
Consider him who endured such opposition from sinful men,
so that you will not grow weary and lose heart.

HEBREWS 12:1-3

I'll never forget October 17, 1989. That's the day a severe earthquake rocked most of northern California, including the San Francisco Bay area where I was participating in the third game of the World Series in Candlestick Park. I vividly remember feeling the strength and power of that quake. The Bay area was devastated and the World Series was delayed several weeks due to the damage.

Before the earthquake hit, I had been scheduled to speak November 1 at an annual prayer breakfast for the city of Santa Cruz. Ticket sales before the earthquake were modest; after the devastation there was standing room only. The citizens of Santa Cruz were frightened and were turning to God for answers.

I will always remember a personal story that a man from the crowd told me that day. He said that fifteen years before the quake, he and his wife had bought their "dream home" in Santa Cruz. They spent fifteen years of their lives putting all their time, money, and efforts into that home. Many times, he chose to stay home on Sunday mornings and work on his house instead of going to church. His home had become his god. But during the earthquake, in a short fifteen seconds, one second for every year he spent worshiping his "god," his home was completely destroyed.

We cannot afford to fix our eyes on what is seen. It doesn't last and it doesn't satisfy. In fifteen seconds it can be all gone. We aren't meant for this world and our hearts will only be broken if we try to possess any little piece of it. So what should we pursue? "Godliness with contentment," Paul suggests. In that there is "great gain," not heartbreaking loss.

So don't break your heart. Go for gain and not for loss. Keep your eye on the Boss, not the ball, and you'll be OK. That's the way they do it in the *real* major leagues.

DAVE DRAVECKY, FORMER SAN FRANCISCO GIANTS PITCHER

Yet Abraham did not waver through unbelief regarding the promise of God, but was strengthened in his faith and gave glory to God, being fully persuaded that God had power to do what he had promised.

ROMANS 4:20, 21

What had produced winning football teams for us over the years has been our willingness to create practice systems and procedures that are aligned with our vision of perfection: *We want to win them all.* Everything I do is to prepare people to perform to the best of their ability. And you do that one day at a time.

DON SHULA, FORMER MIAMI DOLPHINS HEAD COACH

There's something better when you leave here. I invite any of my friends who I'm close to. Just coming to chapel and Bible study—it's a start. Maybe they'll think they do need to give their life to the Lord. I want them to know there's a sacrifice, but they'll be rewarded for it. When it's all over, I want them to be in heaven.

HERSEY HAWKINS, SEATTLE SUPERSONICS GUARD

We fix our eyes not on what is seen,
but on what is unseen. For what is seen is temporary,
but what is unseen is eternal.

2 CORINTHIANS 4:18

Sources

Braker, Bobbie, "Pioneer Spirit" (March 1998), Taken from *Sports Spectrum,* a Christian sports magazine. For subscription information call 1-800-283-8333.

Byrd, Dennis, Excerpt from *Rise & Walk,* © 1993 by Dennis Byrd and Michael D'Orso, Reprinted by permission of HarperCollins Publishers, Inc.

Carvalho, John, "Airing it Out: Wrestling with commitment," (April 1998), Taken from *Sports Spectrum,* a Christian sports magazine. For subscription information call 1-800-283-8333.

Combs, Pat "Action Jackson," (April 1998), Taken from *Sports Spectrum,* a Christian sports magazine. For subscription information call 1-800-283-8333.

Dawson, Andre with Tom Bird, *Today's Heroes: Andre Dawson*, Grand Rapids, MI: ZondervanPublishingHouse, 1994.

Ditchfield, Christin, "The Winning Edge?" (November 1998), Taken from *Sports Spectrum,* a Christian sports magazine. For subscription information call 1-800-283-8333.

Dravecky, Dave with Tim Stafford, *Comeback.* Grand Rapids, MI: ZondervanPublishingHouse, 1990. With C.W. Neal, *The Worth of a Man*, Grand Rapids, MI: ZondervanPublishingHouse, 1996.

Dravecky, Jan and Dave with Steve Halliday, *Do Not Lose Heart*, Grand Rapids, MI: ZondervanPublishingHouse, 1998.

Fryar, Irving, Excerpted from *Sunday is My Day,* © 1997 by Irving Fryar, Used by permission of Multnomah Publishers, Inc.

Gibbs, Jim, "Texas Heat," (October 1998), Taken from *Sports Spectrum,* a Christian sports magazine. For subscription information call 1-800-283-8333.

Green, A.C. with J.C. Webster, *Today's Heroes: A.C. Green*, Grand Rapids, MI: ZondervanPublishingHouse, 1995.

Hubbard, Steve, *Today's Heroes: David Robinson*, Grand Rapids, MI: ZondervanPublishingHouse, 1996.

Jackson, Dean, "Train Up a Child." *Sharing the Victory* (April 1998), 21-22.

Lawson, Steve J., Reprinted from *Men Who Win*. © 1992 by Steve J. Lawson. Used by permission of NavPress, Colorado Springs, CO. All rights reserved. For copies call (800) 366-7788.

Littleton, Mark, *Sports Heroes: Baseball*, Grand Rapids, MI: ZondervanPublishingHouse, 1996, *Sports Heroes: Basketball*, Grand Rapids, MI: ZondervanPublishingHouse, 1995, *Sports Heroes: Basketball 2*, Grand Rapids, MI: ZondervanPublishingHouse, 1996, *Sports Heroes: Soccer*, Grand Rapids, MI: ZondervanPublishingHouse, 1996, *Sports Heroes: Football*, Grand Rapids, MI: ZondervanPublishingHouse, 1995.

Palmeri, Allen, "Dead Men Blocking," (September 1998), Taken from *Sports Spectrum,* a Christian sports magazine. For subscription information call 1-800-283-8333.

Paup, Bryce, Excerpted from *What's Important Now*, © 1997 by Bryce Paup, Used by permission of Multnomah Publishers.

Power for Competing: The Inside Story. Colorado Springs: International Bible Society, 1996.

Ruetggers, Ken, Excerpted from *Home Field Advantage*, © 1995 by Ken Ruettgers, Used by permission of Multnomah Publishers.

Sandrolini, Mike, "No Respect" (May 1998), Taken from *Sports Spectrum,* a Christian sports magazine. For subscription information call 1-800-283-8333.

Semrau, Sue, (April 1999), Taken from *Sports Spectrum,* a Christian sports magazine. For subscription information call 1-800-283-8333.

Shula, Don & Ken Blanchard, *Everyone's a Coach*, Grand Rapids, MI: ZondervanPublishingHouse, 1995.

Smith, Charlotte, "Straight Talk with Charlotte Smith," (April 1999), Taken from *Sports Spectrum,* a Christian sports magazine. For subscription information call 1-800-283-8333.

"Taffarel Live!" (June 1998), Taken from *Sports Spectrum,* a Christian sports magazine. For subscription information call 1-800-283-8333.

Trout, Mike, *A Journey to the Heart of America*. Grand Rapids, MI: ZondervanPublishingHouse, 1998.

Umlandt, Mike, "Home Run," (April 1999), Taken from *Sports Spectrum,* a Christian sports magazine. For subscription information call 1-800-283-8333.